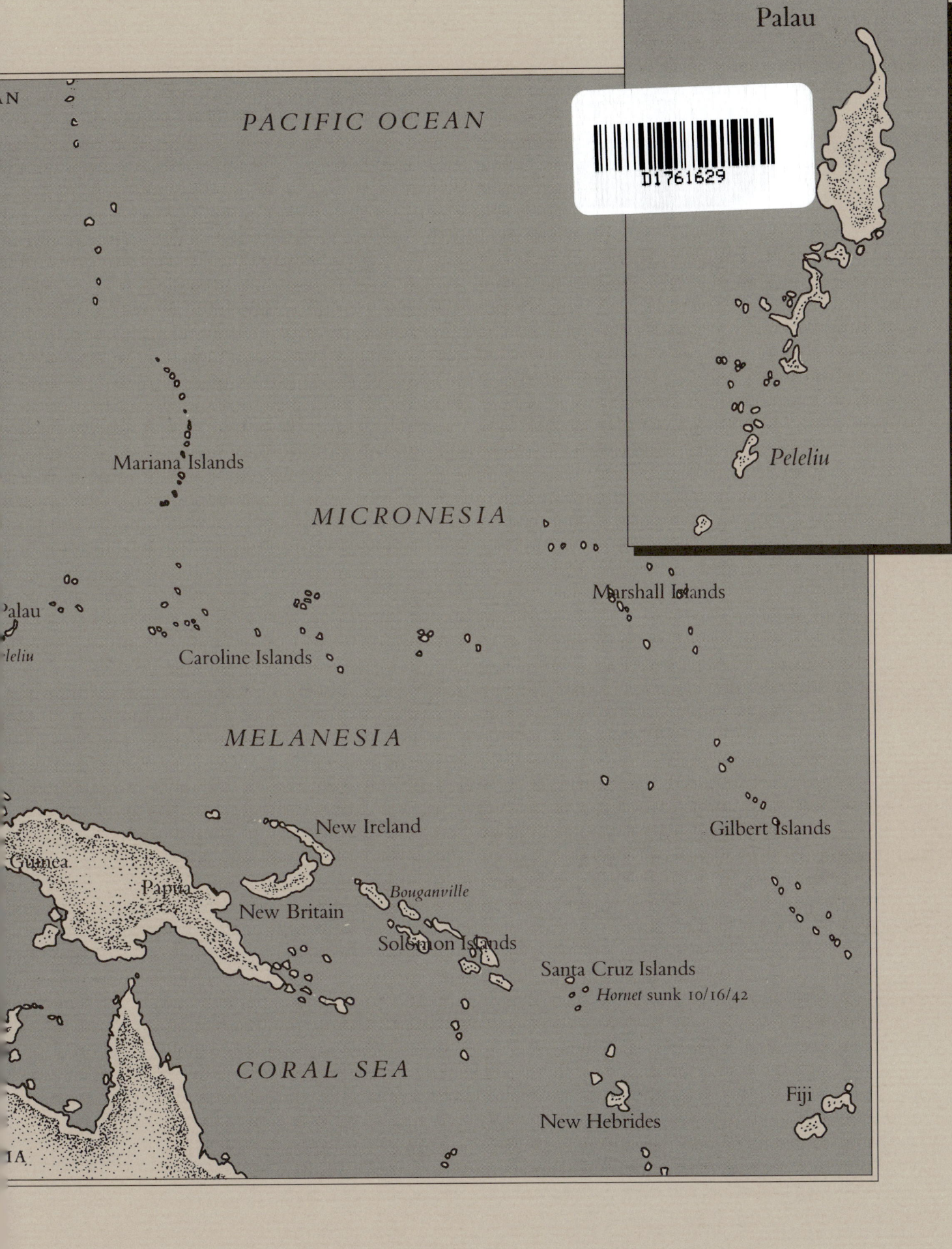

BATTLE STATIONS

TOM LEA
BATTLE STATIONS

A Grizzly from the Coral Sea
Peleliu Landing

Illustrations by the author
Introduction by Al Lowman

STILL POINT PRESS • DALLAS

Copyright © 1988 Tom Lea

"A Grizzly from the Coral Sea" by Tom Lea. Copyright 1944 by Carl Hertzog. Reprinted by permission of Vivian Hertzog and the author.

"Peleliu Landing" by Tom Lea. Copyright 1945 by Tom Lea. Reprinted by permission of the author.

This book may not be reproduced, in whole or in part, in any form (beyond that copying permitted by Sections 107 and 108 of the 1976 U.S. Copyright Law and except by reviewers for the public press) without written permission from the author and publishers.

Library of Congress Cataloging-in-Publication Data
Lea, Tom, 1907–
    [Grizzly from the Coral Sea]
    Battle Stations / Tom Lea ; illustrations by the author ; introduction by Al Lowman.
      xii + 75 pp. 21.59 × 27.94 cm.
    Reprint (1st work). Originally published: El Paso, Tex. : C. Hertzog, 1944.
    Reprint (2nd work). Originally published: El Paso : C. Hertzog, 1945.
    Contents: Introduction —. A Grizzly from the Coral Sea — Peleliu Landing.
    ISBN 0-933841-07-8 : $19.95
    1. Lea, Tom, 1907–   . 2. World War, 1939–1945—Campaigns—Palau.
3. World War, 1939–1945—Personal narratives, American. 4. War correspondents—United States—Biography.   5. Palau—History.
I. Lea, Tom, 1907–   Peleliu Landing. 1988. II. Title.
D767.99.P4L39 1988
940.54'26—dc19
                                          88-19176
                                            CIP

Contents

Introduction—
Eyewitness to Battle
vii

A Grizzly from the Coral Sea
3

Peleliu Landing
27

Eyewitness to Battle

World War II resides permanently in the history books, the film archives, and in the memories of the men and women who lived through those turbulent years from 1939 to 1945. Having spent my own childhood in the long shadow of that war, there are two images that are ineradicable in my mind's eye. Both appeared initially in wartime issues of *Life* magazine. The first is a Cartier-Bresson photograph of a not quite middle-aged little Frenchman standing along the Champs Élysées in Paris, tears streaming down his round cheeks as Nazi invaders rumble into the City of Light. The other is Tom Lea's painting of a young marine at his moment of death on Peleliu Island. An exploding shell has caused the left half of his face and torso to dissolve in blood. The look on what remains of that face seems at once disbelieving and apologetic, as if he had failed in a mission. Lea himself described it differently: "The most terrifying look of abject patience I have ever seen." Although the marine is still on his feet, he will take only another step or two.

For those who allow their thoughts to dwell on these two

images, a deep emotional response is evoked: the Frenchman mourning the loss of freedom, the marine dying half a world away to restore it. Two faces of tragedy and, of the two, the marine's fate more haunting.

World War II in the South Pacific was like no other in which American forces had fought, a seemingly endless succession of sea battles and naval invasions. The islands involved were geographically obscure until bloodshed brought them momentarily to prominence. In the early forties the folks back home would be searching every few days for new pinpoints on their maps, often in vain, because few households had sufficiently detailed maps or atlases. Almost invariably these pinpoints were associated with sacrifice, heroism, and God-forsaken terrain.

With western Europe at war and America preoccupied with the threat of Nazi Germany, Imperial Japan had seen opportunity to promote its own territorial expansion by advancing on European and American interests throughout the Malay Archipelago, which occupies Pacific waters north of Australia and south of China and Japan. First, they had to prevent America's interference by crippling its naval armada concentrated at Pearl Harbor and its airpower in the Philippines. Japanese success in both endeavors on December 7, 1941, is well remembered.

Almost simultaneously two invasion forces were mounted from Japanese-held territory in southern China. The first, from Formosa Island, landed on Philippine soil two days after the December 7 attack. The second began a long counterclockwise sweep from the south China mainland through French Indo-China, down the Malay Peninsula, and into the Dutch East Indies with its rich oil reserves. The Japanese then advanced eastward into New Guinea and the Solomon Islands, at which point they occupied practically the entire Malay Archipelago and posed a critical threat to Australia. By April 1942 victory seemed in their grasp, but in early May they were dealt a setback in the four-day Battle of the Coral Sea, between the northeast coast of Australia and the eastern Solomons. As a result of this action, the threat to Australia was greatly diminished.

But a new sense of urgency arose when the Allies learned that the Japanese were hastening construction of an airbase at Guadalcanal in the eastern Solomons. The Allies launched their first major offensive there on August 7, 1943, and won a costly but vital victory. After months of adverse news, Americans had something to feel good about.

The naval battles in the eastern Solomons raged at varying levels of intensity for the next two months. On September 15, Japanese submarines sank the United States aircraft carrier *Wasp*. As an artist-correspondent for *Life*, Tom Lea was there, watching from a signal bridge of the fleet's only other operational carrier, *Hornet*. His experience aboard *Hornet* provided the setting for *A Grizzly from the Coral Sea*, the account of a developing friendship that was later cemented with a gift of a silver coin embossed with the head of a grizzly bear.

Lea stayed with *Hornet* another five weeks, until October 22, then made his way to Pearl Harbor. There, Admiral Chester Nimitz himself told Lea that *Hornet* had been sunk only thirty-six hours after his departure. Lea's story of the car-

EYEWITNESS TO BATTLE

rier and his lucky coin was first published in 1944 in a limited edition of 295 copies by his printer friend, Carl Hertzog of El Paso.

The Japanese abandoned the Guadalcanal campaign in February 1943, and their military operations became primarily defensive. By the middle of that year the Allied high command had decided that ultimately the Pacific war would be carried to the Japanese mainland by way of Micronesia, those groups of islands—the Gilberts, the Marshalls, the Carolines, the Marianas, the Palaus—that lie north of the equator and east of the Philippines.

In late November 1943 American forces began leapfrogging toward the Philippines with Japan as their eventual goal. They paid a steep price at such places as Tarawa, Kwajalein, Eniwetok, Saipan, and Guam. By mid-September 1944 the Americans were poised to assault the Japanese on the Palau Islands five hundred miles east of Mindanao, the southern anchor of the Philippines.

Tom Lea returned to the South Pacific in time to participate in the invasions of the Palau Islands, where the Japanese had built an airfield, one the Allies needed to support the Philippine operation. The Palau invasion occurred at Peleliu Island. Lea went in between the first and second assault waves, then returned to his ship after a day and a half to record the action in stark and poignant sketches—in his words, "before my hand steadied." He had been, as he later recalled, "so close to eternity that the owl's hoot was plainly audible from the other side of Hell."

In these scenes from Peleliu a remarkable artist has given

EYEWITNESS TO BATTLE

us the visual counterpart to the sense of combat that we derive from reading the literature of Tolstoi, Stendahl, and Stephen Crane. Eleven oil paintings based on the Peleliu drawings appeared in the June 11, 1945, issue of *Life*. About the same time, Carl Hertzog made a stunning book of the original sketches and had it bound in marine dungaree cloth with its familiar herringbone twill. Here the emotional impact—the inspired integration of artwork, vivid prose, design, and production—renders *Peleliu Landing* one of the finest examples of bookmaking ever seen in the Southwest.

Summarizing the Pacific war in an effort to put Tom Lea's experience in a geographical and chronological context does not imply that the battles mentioned were the only ones that mattered. Artists in addition to Lea were covering equally desperate, equally courageous engagements elsewhere in the Pacific as well as the European theaters. Lea has described the artist-correspondent as

> a roving feature story writer, but in graphics instead of words. . . . He transmitted his work to his editor's desk by bringing it back himself, when it was ready. . . . To get back with his own pictures in his own hand, he had to learn to make his own way. Nobody made it for him. . . . To get where he wanted to go and see what he wanted to see, he eventually learned to step lively, travel light, keep his eyes wide open and his mouth mostly shut, listen, bear a hand with a smile, and hope for the best.

Unquestionably, Tom Lea not only hoped for the best, he gave his best, too. And so did the fighting men and women he portrayed. Not long ago one of the New York literati characterized World War II as "the last good war," meaning, one supposes, that it was the last in which Americans all agreed that we were clearly on the side of right. Men still die nobly, even heroically, in causes far less just. No doubt they die bearing the same expressions of disbelief, apology, and abject patience.

After his experience at Peleliu, Tom Lea returned to Texas and summed up his thoughts:

> I came home to El Paso not trying to understand the providence that brought me back. I felt that I had no real right to be home. I felt that I was not there, that I could never be there, back home and within its blessing, until I was finished recording the testimony to which I was sworn as an eyewitness, for others as well as myself: what battle is and how it looks when you are there.

AL LOWMAN
San Marcos, Texas

A Grizzly from the Coral Sea

"B-E-R-I—*G-A-N spells Berrigan!*"

"You left out an R, Berrigan. You're drunk."

"*G-A-N spells Berrigan.*

"How many *Gombeis* did we drink anyway?"

"I don't know. That fellow from *Tass* has some very active drinking companions. Wow. . . Say, Berry, I'm drunk myself."

"Very good to be well skronked. Specially in Chungking. Specially in the rain. Specially when Joe's boys have an anniversary with free drinks and take Kiev the same day. If I could just get cockeyed ever time it rained, I'd be drunk all the time in dear old, dear old bloody buggerin' Chungking."

"Lookout for that puddle. Jeesis, Berry, am I going to have to carry you? Why in hell did those Russians rent an embassy on top up such a greasy wet hill?"

"Who was the blonde with the guy wearing all the braid up there? Um. It does take braid, in China's war torn capital. Hell.

"*G-A-N spells Berrrr-igun!*"

"Are we going back to that stinking Press Hostel? I feel

too good to crawl back into that rabbit hutch with all our dear colleagues. They remind me of guys on a life raft."

"All right. Let's don't go to the Press Hostel. Let's don't ever go back. Let's sing. We'll ask the Old Man for transportation to the Chin Hills."

At the bottom of the hill the cobbled street was swollen with hordes of the poor Chinese moving along in their gray and blue and seedy black like the current of the *Yangtze*. The two American uniforms were like brown chips caught in the snaggy eddies of the gray torrent. Gray mud splashed them and the cold rain slanted down.

"Did you see the sores on that coolie's head? Woof! I never get used to it. That old devil probably rubs his head with rat tail salve at night and figures he's doing fine."

"What really gets me about China is the smell. Rain doesn't help it a bit. I guess it can't be washed away. You're a man of words. How'd you describe what we're smelling? I'd ruin my brushes painting that smell. So how would you string words together to make it, Berry? So people that never smelled China could get a whiff."

"That's a matter only for the real live nose, my friend. Oly-factry. Smells. Smells compounded from dirt that crawls and bodies that stink. Big fecal doin's, brother. And reasty nidors of cortile corruption. Sour smoke from the trash bins of hell."

"Not as good as the nose, Berry, but pretty good. Fecal is the word."

"Let's sing:
*There's a troop ship that's leaving Bombay,
Bound for old Blighty Shore—*"

"This walking and this rain is taking the edge off the Russian hospitality. My wool blouse smells like Calcutta gin when it's wet."

"Don't you wish you were down on *Per Diem* Hill now?"

"Let's go some place to get dry—and some tea, that hot green tea. But not the Press Hostel, that hole, that crying shame of a dump. I would like a Martini with a onion, in that little French place on 51st Street. Hey, Berry, how would you like to be walking up Fifth Avenue in this rain?"

"Nuts. . . . Say, I think I know where we might get a little steak. How would you like some steak and some hot tea?"

"Don't give me that. You know how I'm waiting for that fine Chinese chow tonight at the hostel, if I don't lose a finger under your chopsticks."

"No kidding. Teddy and Bill said they got a steak. Chinese-American Institute of Cultural Relations. Honest to God that's the name of the place. There's a big sign. They might have steak. How about that?"

There were four steps leading up from the swollen river of gray Chinese in the crooked street. Inside the door, the Chinese-American Institute of Cultural Relations smelled like tung oil. The restaurant was at the rear. Most of the tables were occupied by young Chinese in spectacles and western clothes, treating their long-gowned girl friends to western chow.

Berry grinned and whispered. "Never mind, pal. Their gowns are slit high up the side sometimes but they always wear pants. Just like home, or is it. We'll ask about steak."

The little waiter understood about the steak and tea and nodded his head. "Flench flies?" he asked.

"What did I tell you," said Berry. "Best cultural relations I ever met up with, I hope. Tell you later. Say, have you got some money along?"

A big wad of 100-yuan inflation bank notes came out of a side pants pocket. A Zippo lighter and an American half dollar came with it, and lay there on the table.

"Here's old Kung's signature on this bill. His autograph is prettier than his puss I'd say—"

A GRIZZLY FROM THE CORAL SEA

"What in the hell is this trick half dollar? Is it real or something you can always flip heads with?"

"It's real. It's my bear. My grizzly bear."

The food came and it wasn't bad. Somebody had slaughtered an ox all right: it was beefsteak and there were french fries along with it even if they were a little limp and rancid. And the tea was fine, hot and aromatic in the little clean white bowls.

The Chinese-American Institute of Cultural Relations seemed rather mellow in fact. Berry was wiping up the last of the gravy with his last french fry when he asked, "What about that trick four bits again? You a coin collector?"

"Nope. But I think a lot of this one. It's my lucky piece."

"I never saw one like it before."

Over in the corner three American GIs—two Pfcs and a buck sergeant from HQ—were quietly digesting their pieces of the ox and staring without giving a damn at the big squiggled characters in the cultural mottoes on the wall. The rain outside pounded on a little steamy window above their heads.

"Where'd you get this?" Berry asked.

"It's a grizzly from the Coral Sea."

"How do you mean?"

"It's complicated, and I might get eloquent and that would be bad."

"Not bad. Good. This is an eloquent occasion. Steak in Chungking. Tell me about the bear."

"O.K., Berry. Look at those GIs over there in the corner. Sad sacks. I guess Americans are the homesickest soldiers in the war. I know that often I'm the homesickest correspondent. I don't want to be here any more than those GIs do, me prowling around the world getting the hell scared out of me. I'm a peace-loving picture painter with a home and a wife and a boy, and the mountain I was born under is right out my studio window.

"A lot of times, like last night when you drunken forlorn clucks were warbling across the compound and the rain was pouring and that 3-watt light bulb of mine was murking my lonesome rabbit hutch, I get very low and I cuss the war and all the bastards who cause wars and send so many guys to so many places where they don't belong.

"I hate those professional Texans I meet everywhere yelling about Texas. (You're from California, aren't you, Berry? They're damn near as bad.) But I was born in West Texas. I grew up there and I live there now. Yelling 'Yip-Pee' in front of strangers doesn't satisfy my feelings in the matter. Anyway—"

"But what about that coin? It's a California commemorative half dollar."

"I was coming to that. I was going to tell you about the bear, the grizzly from the Coral Sea. It's a silver bear I carry in my pocket, and California has nothing to do with it. You asked me what it was and I have to get at it the way I'm doing."

Berry was a nice guy. He didn't say "Roger." He just grinned and said, "Please go on."

"It was right after the *Hornet* boys had hit Bougainville. We ran up close one rainy October morning and caught the Japs with their pants and anchors down. It was pretty good. At that time those waters were strictly Tojo and we were right under the noses of any land-based stuff that wanted a crack.

"It was tense and touchy those days. The marines on Guadalcanal were getting kicked around, and the navy was having no picnic. In the middle of September when we joined the *Wasp* force hoping for a crack at the Jap carrier forces farther north, the Japs very neatly caught us with a submarine attack. There were torpedoes all over the ocean that afternoon. When the smoke had cleared, the *Hornet* was the only U.S. carrier fit for fighting in the whole Pacific.

"Our admiral and our skipper were on a spot—not that they didn't pray for a chance to sock something—but they were on a spot. They were taking big chances right in the Japs' teeth, and in doing that risking our only carrier, our only movable airport, desperately needed in the Solomons deal. Like I said, it was tense and touchy. The strain of doing a job, knowing the tragic cost of not doing it right, took hold of everybody from the admiral on down. Nerves got ragged. We got kind of jumpy. A radical change of course in the middle of the night brought sound sleepers right out of their bunks with flashlights and shoes in their heavy hands. In our purely private emotional lives none of us ever blanked out the sight of the *Wasp* that afternoon at the foot of that column of smoke. It was a constant reminder.

"All twenty-four hours of the day before the one I'm going to talk about we had been at general quarters. We socked Bougainville and then ran out, south and southwest. So far, the Japs had not sent bombers for us. We figured they must have known where we were from their snoopers which our fighters had shot down, but not before the Mitsubishis had time to radio our position and course. So we were definitely expecting.

"Lunch in the wardroom was a luxury after the long general quarters, but the atmosphere was hardly one of genial relaxation. A laugh, when there was one, was a little strident. Conversation was apt to turn to argument. People chewed their blocked beef stew absentmindedly. Two department heads sat at table with big sweat rings under their arms. The Exec had his meal interrupted twice by messengers.

"Eddie Harp, the chaplain, sat next to me. I said, 'Eddie if I ever hit a beach again, the first thing I'm going to do is get plastered.' He looked owlish through his glasses and answered, 'You have my ecclesiastical sanction.'

"Across the table sat Herbert Jackson, Communications, a strictly professional lieutenant commander, Annapolis, '29; but also strictly a warm and humane man. Something like you, Berry. That's why I'm telling you about the bear.

"Herb had a round face and a good-humored eye. He was filling a certain conversational void with a disagreeable subject, which was the long lack of mail. 'All I got in the last mail,' he was saying, 'was a coin catalogue. Interesting but damn impersonal. . . . Say when are you coming down to see those coins I have?' he suddenly asked me.

"'Anytime you say. I'd like to see them. Herb, the *Hornet* is a hell of a place to store valuable coins, if I may say so. If I'm going to see them, I just might ought to hurry some.'

"'Hm. Let's knock off after we're through eating. I'll break them out . . . like to look at them again myself. Of course, I haven't got my real collection aboard here. These are just some Greek and Roman pieces I wanted to study when we left Norfolk.' The surgeon sitting next to me stirred uncomfortably, afraid Mr. Jackson might start rocking the old hobby-horse again.

"The wardroom was emptying, the mess boys clattering the china, when I followed Jackson down the passageway to his room on the same deck. He initialed some flimsies on the board by his door, telephoned Radio Central, and then unlocked his metal desk drawer and brought out a nice mahogany box. Opened, it had little black velvet trays in it, and the coins were sitting in little black velvety wells cut to their various sizes.

"I don't know anything about coins, but some of them were beautiful. Herb handled them and named them for me. The way he held them in his hand I knew what he thought of them. There were some little gold and silver pieces with horses and chariots. Herb was partial to the ones with galleys, triremes. But I liked the little owls from Athens; they were wonderful. Professor Jackson was explaining about the big tits on Astarte when some mech must have dropped a monkey wrench on the iron hangar deck right over our heads.

"'Goddammit!' yelled Herb. Both of us had jumped, and some of the coins had fallen to the deck. 'Why can't those people be careful. A thing like that is irritating.'

"'These animals, Herb, the lucky signs on coins of Athens and Corinth, they remind me of the Indians at home. Ever know anything about Indian medicine, fetishes in the medicine bag?'

"Herb was a Texan, but he was a town and farm boy from around Waco, and he said he didn't know a thing about Indians or chousing cows or West of the Pecos.

"'Well,' I said, 'every Indian warrior carried an animal fetish in his medicine bag, a part or a symbol of the animal that was his secret medicine, his power, that was revealed to him during the lonely dreams of his novitiate fasting. That animal was connected with his power in this life and the next. It represented a warrior's potence to cope with the mysteries of life, of war, of nature, of death. It was quite a thing. This owl reminds me of the Sioux. Sometimes I wish I'd been an Indian in the great days with horses on the plains. When I was a kid I dreamed of it. And you know, I even knew, always, my medicine animal if I'd been an Indian.'

"I let him ask me what it would be and I had just opened my mouth to say when the boatswain's pipe screeched through the loudspeaker in the passageway, and the boatswain's mate of the watch rasped, and the tone of his voice was not routine, '*GENERAL QUARTERS! GENERAL QUARTERS! ALL HANDS! MAN YOUR BATTLE STATIONS!*' and the general alarm screamed its penetrating sonic scream.

"Herb slapped shut the mahogany box, jammed it in the desk drawer, locked it, grabbed his life jacket and tin hat, and I said 'See you later!'

"I had to run about forty yards of crooked passageway and up two decks to my room for my gear and my sketch books and then climb over eighty steps on narrow crowded ladders to the signal bridge before the bulkheads locked me in. Brother I was in a hurry.

"A general quarters like that is something on a carrier expecting trouble. It's something everybody has half wanted and half dreaded for a long time. It's like being perched right on the

bulls-eye just before the shooting starts. There's nothing funny about guys hurrying to stations carrying their gear and maybe stuffing into a pocket what they have figured they will take with them over the side. You can hear over two thousand pairs of feet pounding the iron decks and ladders, going to the places they'll be when something happens, while the ship heels over on fifty-dollar turns changing course. You can hear the big bulkhead doors banging shut and being dogged down and the damage control boys slamming their long wrenches to valves on the lines.

"Topside the airedales on the flight deck are running and pushing their hearts out getting the Wildcats aft ready to launch immediately to augment the Combat Air Patrol. The gunners are loosening up their guns, wiggling them like stubby fingers across their full traverses. Up in the island, the brains and nerves of the ship above the flight deck, there is a cold continual measured passage of orders that flow to the remotest corners of the ship. The air officer puts on his iron hat without taking his eyes from his study of the flight log. Radio Central tunes new frequencies. The admiral stands on the inboard side of his bridge, squinting and frowning past the port quarter. The captain steps from the wheelhouse chewing an unlighted cigar while a boatswain shuts the battle ports. In the charthouse the old chief quartermaster stows his own private knotted emergency line behind a handy transom, ready for going over the side. 'These may be tough times, sonny.'

"All around the carrier the cruisers and cans are closing in, forming the emergency protective screen, ready for the circling war dance around their queen. Starting-cartridges pop at the command '*START ENGINES!*' on the flight deck, where the fighters' propellers begin to turn with a roar, and the carrier turns into the wind to launch them.

"And up on the signal bridge where my station was, in the whistling wind at the top of the island, the signalmen, quick-change artists, are going nuts with their popping flags in

the windy sunlight, and their click-clacking shutters on the signal lamps. The admiral is talking to his ships.

"Well, the Japs didn't come in on the *Hornet*. They knew all about us, too. There was plenty of time for them to use a radio before our fighters knocked down a two-engined snooper back on our port quarter. Close in, too. We saw it explode in midair with one of those bright pink flashes. When it hit the water it sent up a long column of brown smoke over our fantail. Silver Emerson knocked another one down a few minutes later. (I did a portrait of Silver. He's dead now.)

"We never knew why the Japs didn't close on us. We were the real target, but they didn't close. They took a convoy of supply ships going to Guadalcanal instead. They hit and ran before our fighters could get out that far. Maybe that bunch of Japs wasn't eager enough for a job like the *Hornet*. Anyway they hit the convoy and went home.

"The augmented air patrol buzzed around until they had to come in for gas. But we stayed at general quarters. The Old Man figured the Japs still had daylight time to hit us from the air. And he was sure all the Jap subs knew about us by now, from the snoopers. So he kept the *Hornet* buttoned up, and us at our stations.

"It gets tedious as hell standing around on an iron deck with a let-down feeling. I think adrenalin gives you a kind of hangover. Ever notice that, Berry?

"Anyway, at general quarters you have to stand around and your feet hurt and you're thirsty. We were dopey and gritty-eyed that day to start with.

"About 1730 the bomb elevators opened up from the flight deck and we could see the mess boys down there handing up the buckets of doughnuts and coffee for everybody topside. The chief signalman sent two boys down for our share and they came up with our supper, smoking coffee that put curly hair on your teeth, and damp doughnuts. They passed around some cartons of candy bars too, broken out of ship's stores.

"Word passed that the ship would stay buttoned up all

night, and we groaned and kissed goodbye any thoughts of our nice soft sacks below decks.

"I never saw anything like the sunset that night. It was spooky. The sea was almost flat calm, but the sky was banked high with thunderheads and low curtains of rain. The color of the sunset was the most intense I have ever seen. And it was in reverse. Instead of a dark sea and colored sky, it was the other way around. The sky was a brooding purple, like a bruise, and the ocean a bloody red. The red bounced up and fired our faces against the dark sky. There was something eerie about that sea of blood. Bergquist, the signalman whose folks had sailed for generations, frankly didn't like that sunset. And Ensign James Day, the young lawyer from Denver, walked out of the coding room and felt the same way.

"Herb Jackson came topside from Radio Central to see how his signalmen were, and we stood there and watched the bloody sea turn to ink. Suddenly in the west I spotted the new horned moon, a thin fingernail of fire.

"'New moon, Herb.' He was facing aft on the starboard side, and when he looked out abeam he saw the moon over his left shoulder. It was the last new moon he ever saw from the *Hornet*. At that moment, I think he knew it.

"'I don't like what's coming in to the coding room,' he said. 'I didn't like that this afternoon, either. Things aren't shaping the best way. It looks like the Japs are getting ready to send their heavy stuff down to Guadalcanal. Our raid yesterday didn't do much to change their minds.'

"'You mean they're at last bringing out their carriers for a slugfest with us?'

"'Hell no . . . I wish they were. No, I'm talking about battleships and heavy cruisers. I can't figure their carrier plays. Apparently they are waiting for something, I don't know what. The marines are taking a pasting meantime. Our carrier has got to put in more licks. But I don't see how we can hit those battlewagons and cruisers without putting the *Hornet*'s tail in a crack.

"'Oh well. . . . Hello, Puck. Say those were soggy doughnuts you gave us tonight, Mr. Mess Caterer.'

"'I know it, Mr. Jackson. We baked ten thousand of them last night, just in case. They weren't very good, but at least we had something on hand when this came up this afternoon.'

"'I know it. I'm just kidding. When are you going to have us some fried chicken and ice cream?'

"'Well, sir, we're really going to have some the 21st. Birthday party. It seems like a lot longer than that since we were at Norfolk on Commissioning Day, doesn't it, Mr. Jackson?'

"'It does, Puck. Well . . . that chicken and ice cream will be something. Will we have a birthday cake?'

"'Yes sir, with one little pink candle.'

"Lieutenant (senior grade) Puck Pucket, being Mess Caterer and in the Paymaster's department, didn't have specific battle duties. He could pick his own station, and he had chosen the signal bridge so he could always see what was going on—like I had. Puck had a fine mind and a warm heart. He was good company even when your feet hurt at general quarters.

"'You boys going to make yourselves comfortable on the bridge tonight?' asked Jackson, and without waiting for an answer added, 'See you later when my desk is clean.'

"So the sun went down and the clouds began to clear to

show the stars, the strange stars I never saw when I looked up from a bedroll in the *Bosque Redondo* by the Rio Grande. Puck and I didn't say much. We leaned against the iron splinter-shield on the gun-director platform, and felt the dark sea, and the sky, and the war.

"An hour later, when Herb Jackson reappeared up the dark ladder from the navigation bridge, he joined us quietly and we just stood there against the damp iron, looking into the darkness. We were at ease with each other. Down on the flight deck we could make out the sprawling shapes of the tired airedales, sleeping on their life jackets by the planes. Not far from where we stood, the signalmen were huddled on the step just forward of the flag bags, talking in low slow voices. There was a hush over everything that seemed to give the huge dark *Hornet* a mysterious destination.

"Far below, the black water seethed as it slid past. On that leg of her zigzag course the *Hornet* was running before the wind, and it made the air strangely still. Stack gas hung forward of the stack and made us cough. The great black ship moved only to the vibration of her screws—there was not the slightest pitch or roll to the invisible sea. The black shapes of war, the metal rigging and superstructures, seemed unfamiliar against the unfamiliar stars in the clearing sky.

"Our minds drew together. We voyaged to the mysterious destination, each separately with all we remembered and all we desired; but together too, as if we shared the most important thing of all, which we could not have named.

"'You haven't told me yet what animal you'd be carrying in your sea bag if you were a Sioux sailor,' said Herb.

"'A grizzly. A grizzly bear from up near the timberline

would be my medicine. Getting back to those coins, Herb, is there one with a bear on it?'

"'Oh, there must be. Yes, I remember. There is. Of course the bear was the strongest brute the Indians knew. Is that why he's your medicine?'

"'I don't know. Maybe that's the kind of medicine dream a mild and timid guy would always have. But it wasn't just his brute force. Somehow he came to represent the things I feel about the country where I was born. Things like that are never logical. The grizzly was the flesh and warm blood, the counterpart in creatures to old Mount Franklin, the stone-sided mountain at home . . . I don't know . . . Tonight I'd like to see a grizzly bear. Just the sight of a grizzly bear would be good for—for this. Sounds nuts to you and Puck. War happy.'

"'No,' said Puck, 'I'm a sailor. There's really a kind of a luck in your life to have something like that.'

"'Maybe I like bears because of the picture over my bed at home when I was a little kid. It was a grizzly high on the rocks looking far out over a winding river where buffalo watered. When I was old enough to read, I found the picture was entitled "Before the White Man Came." I remember waking up in the mornings and seeing that old grizzly standing watch. He was a friend.

"'Again, maybe the reason I like a bear is because of Old Scarface, the grizzly hero of the stories my father used to make up for my brother Joe and me before we went to bed. There'll never be anything as good as those stories in all my life again. They were about Old Scarface's adventures with two little cubs he was raising. They used to have the damnedest scrapes

with bee trees and hunters and avalanches, but everything came out all right because Old Scarface understood the land they lived in.

"'He taught the cubs all the things they had to learn about living, from early springtime when they woke up thin and hungry and came out into the light, until late fall when the yellow aspen leaves were gone and they found the wonderful cave that was so warm and quiet and slept while the wind howled and the fir trees gathered the white snow like Christmas morning.'

"The *Hornet* swung round on the other leg of her zigzag. Suddenly the wind sang in the foretop, whipped our clothes against us, carried the stack gas aft, seemed even to brighten the stars. The Southern Cross stood high and dead ahead.

"'Gentlemen, we are under unfamiliar stars. So far from home we cannot see the greatest bear of all, Ursa Major of the Northern Sky.'

"Well, Berry, it turned out that my destination was different from Herb's and different from Puck's. The next two weeks were rough and tough. The Japs brought their heavy stuff down to Guadalcanal and damn near blew the marines off the beach. *Hornet* planes were about the only thing the United States had in the air over the Solomons for a day or two. Admiral Scott took his cruisers in one night—that was the Battle of Cape Esperance that saved the Solomons for us—and the Japs got hurt and toned down some. Radio Tokyo was blabbing how the Imperial Navy had been given orders to get the *Hornet*, but they wouldn't bring their carriers down, and the land-based stuff never got together for a full-dress job on us. So we pulled out a little south to fuel.

"It looked like the *Hornet*, according to the dope the skipper and the admiral would give me, was in for some more waiting before the Japs tangled again. My drawings were done, I wasn't making a career of the *Hornet* (I'd been on her more than two months), so I decided to leave her. I had no way in this world of knowing that very moment the Japs were assembling four carrier task forces for a showdown with the *Hornet*.

"I was in the wardroom for the birthday party. The thin fingernail of a moon Herb Jackson saw over his left shoulder had waxed, grown full, and begun to wane that morning, just before dawn, when I stood on the bridge of another ship and watched the *Hornet* with her birds sleeping peacefully on her moonlit deck move out into the darkness.

"Back at Pearl Harbor after a series of hitchhikes, and some of them misbegotten, too, I was standing by Admiral Nimitz's desk showing him my drawings, and he came to the one of the *Hornet* at dawn. Underneath I had inscribed a quotation from Deuteronomy, seventh chapter, twentieth verse: *Moreover the Lord thy God shall send the hornet among them, until they that are left, and hide themselves from thee, be destroyed.*

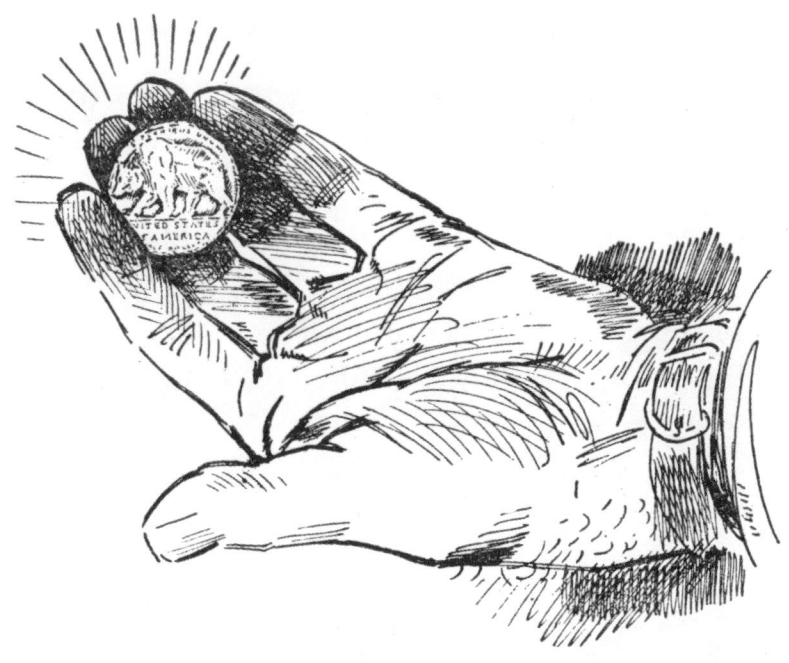

"Admiral Nimitz looked a long time, then turned his head and said, 'Something has happened to the *Hornet*.' That's how I found out.

"When I got home, Mount Franklin was still there. I remember standing by the window at sundown staring at a last summer's bird nest in the top of a leafless tree, wishing for a day to spend thinking about the bird that built that nest, about the sky it lived in, and how the leaves were in the summertime. But the next morning, of course, I was painting the *Hornet*.

"Not long after I got home the postman delivered a heavy envelope. Outside was the mailing sticker of a coin dealer in New York. Inside was the silver bear. Nothing else.

"It was from Herb Jackson. Puck had been killed on the signal bridge about ten feet from where we talked about the bear."

"The hot China tea has vanquished the hot China wine," Berry was saying. "Goddam you. I wish I had a bear and a mountain."

The two American uniforms again were like brown chips caught in the snaggy eddies of the gray torrent of Chinese on the cobbled street. The silver bear rubbed against the signature of H. H. Kung and went up the hill to the Compound gate and the Press Hostel in the rain.

Peleliu Landing

This is not a page from a history book, not an account of a battle. It is the simple narrative of an experience in battle; like combat itself such a narrative is bound to be personal, confused, benumbed and in its deepest sense lonely. D-morning, 15 September, 1944, I landed on Peleliu Island, about fifteen minutes after the first troops hit the beach, with marines under command of Captain Frank Farrell, Headquarters Company, Seventh Regiment. I remained with Farrell and his men under fire for the first thirty-two hours of the assault. As a LIFE War Artist my purpose in going ashore was to record the United States Marines in combat. On the beach I found it impossible to do any sketching or writing; my work there consisted of trying to keep from getting killed and trying to memorize what I saw and felt under fire. On the evening of D-plus-one I returned to a naval vessel offshore where I could record in my sketchbook the burden of this memory. Before my hand steadied I put down the words and pictures that compose this book. The narrative is printed here as I first wrote it except for minor chronological re-arrangement. The sketches are untouched.

MY WATCH said 0340 when I woke up on the blacked-out weatherdeck below the bridge. Barefooted and in my skivvies, I got off my cot and stood by the rail rubbing grit from my eyes. Dead ahead, framed between the forward kingposts, there was flickering light on the black horizon. Sick yellow balls of fire flashed low in the clouds like heat lightning, but continuous. It was the navy shelling Peleliu with the final punch before we landed. The black silhouette of a seaman on watch by the rail turned to me and said, "Them Japs are catching hell for breakfast."

Dawn came dim with low overcast. In the first gray light I saw the sea filled with an awe-inspiring company of strangers to our troop ships. Out to the horizon in every direction were lean men-of-war, fat transports, stubby landing craft, gathered around us like magic in the growing light. It was D-day.

We ate our last meal together, dressed in baggy green dungarees, on the plank benches of the troop officers' mess. We washed the food down our dry throats with big mugs of coffee, and put all the oranges in our pockets. Getting up to go, Captain Farrell repeated his instructions for Martin and me, the two correspondents, "Be at number three net, starboard side, at 0600."

Growing dawn had brought the ship violently to life. Power winches rumbled, hoisting out landing craft over the side. The marines, after long captivity in their crowded holds, moved at last to their stations by the rail, battle gear buckled, the last oil in the gun, the last whet to the knife. I felt some almost palpable spirit walking the emptying holds and passageways and along the crowded decks, with a word for every man.

In the corner where I kept my gear I checked it carefully and finally. There was the belt with the two filled canteens, first-aid kit and long black-bladed knife; and the pack with the poncho and shovel, the gloves, headnet and K-ration, the water-proofed cigarettes and matches and candy bar—and my sketchbook and pencils and camera and films wrapped in the target balloon. All set. I checked my pockets for my watch and identification wrapped in rubbers—and my grizzly coin for luck.

Martin and I buckled our belts, slung our packs and put on our helmets. Inching along through the marines, we found Farrell and his men standing shoulder to shoulder with all their gear on the jampacked main deck near the rail over number three net. The main deck looked queer without the landing craft that had loomed overhead on the long convoy days, making shade for marine card games. Now these boats were down in the water ready for the loads.

"Free boat two," bellowed the squawkbox on the bridge and Farrell said, "That's us. Let's go."

We gave a hitch to our packs, hoisted our legs over the rail and went down the rope net, down the scaly side of our sea-bitten ship by swinging handgrips and tricky footholds between the swaying knots, down to where the bobbing net met the pitching deck of our little iron tub. When we were loaded the coxswain gunned our engine in a blue stink of smoke and we cast off.

Our ship seemed to fall away from us and grow small as we moved out; there was a kind of finality about leaving it. Yet final or not, there was relief in action, and release from morbid imagination. For a moment we even partook of the gaiety of our bobbing tub on the foam-tracked sea. Emotions of an hour ago seemed suddenly unimportant as we looked back at the transport and remembered the parting words we posted on the bulletin board in the ship's officers' wardroom:

A MESSAGE OF THANKS

From: Marines aboard *U.S.S. Repulsive*
To: Officers and Men aboard *U.S.S. Repulsive*

1. It gives us great pleasure at this time to extend our sincere thanks to all members of the crew for their kind and considerate treatment of Marines during this cruise.
2. We non-combatants realize that the brave and stalwart members of the crew are winning the war in the Pacific. You Navy people even go within ten miles of a Japanese island, thereby risking your precious lives. Oh how courageous you are! Oh how our piles bleed for you.
3. Because of your actions during this voyage it is our heartfelt wish that:
   a. The *U.S.S. Repulsive* receives a Jap torpedo immediately after debarkation of all troops.

b. The crew of the *U.S.S. Repulsive* is stranded on Beach Orange Three where Marine units which sailed aboard the ship may repay in some measure the good fellowship extended by the crew and officers during the trip.

4. In conclusion we Marines wish to say to all you dear, dear boys in the Navy: "Bugger you, you bloody bastards!"

Sixteen thousand yards off the beach the LCVPs circled at the sides of their transports, awaiting H-hour. From the air the big vessels must have seemed like a flock of fat ducks with broods of iron ducklings playing ring-around-the-rosy at their mothers' sides.

We circled until 0714 when our signal came to straighten out and head for the transfer line just outside the reef. The circles of iron ducklings suddenly unwound into parallel files of LCVPs gray with the seriousness of war, heading full speed for the flame.

For an hour we plowed toward the beach, the sun above us coming down through the overcast like a silver burning ball. Peleliu was veiled with the smoke of our shelling. New hits against that veil made brown and gray pillars like graceful ghost-trees by Claude Lorrain. As we drew abreast of our battleships and cruisers 1000 yards outside the reef, the sound of their firing changed from dooming booms to the slamming of huge doors.

At 0747 the carrier planes, hundreds of them, noiseless in the roar of gunfire, started pouring death. I counted 96 over my head at once. I saw one flash and fall in a long slow arc of flame.

Over the gunwale of a craft abreast of us I saw a marine, his face painted for the jungle, his eyes set for the beach, his

Going In—First Wave

mouth set for murder, his big hands quiet now in the last moments before the tough tendons drew up to kill.

At 0759 I noticed the amphibious tanks and tractors, the LVTAs and LVTs that would carry us over the reef, being spewed from the maws of LSTs. Sending twin plumes of foam from their tracks aft, they made their way to the tranfer line.

At 0800 the rockets from LCI gunboats flashed pink and soared in flaming curves, by salvos, into a wall of smoke on the beach.

At 0830 we wallowed aft the control boat on the transfer line, the reef a hundred yards ahead, and beyond the edge of the reef 700 yards of green shallow water thick with black niggerheads of coral. The first Jap mortar burst hit just inside the reef as our coxswain worked us up alongside an LVT for transfer. While the two craft bobbed and smashed at each other, we numbly piled ourselves and our gear into the LVT. The coxswain of the LCVP waved, backed his craft clear, and headed seaward.

The iron bulkheads of the LVT came above our heads— we could see only the sky. Farrell climbed on a pile of gear to see out, preparatory to giving our new coxswain the signal for heading in over the reef. Standing on a field radio case forward, I managed to poke my head up so I could see the first wave of LVTs go in. As I watched, the silence came into my consciousness; our shelling had ceased. Only our tank treads churning the water marred the quietness.

Then on the lip of the beach we saw many pink flashes— the Japs, coming out from under our shelling, were opening up with mortar and artillery fire on the first wave. Dead ahead there was a brighter flash. Looking through his binoculars, Farrell told us, "They hit an LVT."

As our coxswain watched the amphitracks toiling through the black obstructions on the reef, I heard him say to Farrell he doubted if it were possible to get us to our precise point on the far right of Beach Orange Three, and Farrell answered, "Well, take us as close as you can."

Mortar bursts began to plume up all over the reef and walk along the edge of the beach. Farrell, who could have waited another hour to take our free boat (not belonging to a specific assault wave) into the beach, abruptly put down his glasses, cupped his hands at the gunner by the coxswain, and bawled, "Let's quit this farting around. Tell him to take us in!"

The clatter of our treads rose to the pitch of a rock crusher and our hell ride began. In that clanking hearse it was impossible to stand without holding on to something, impossible to sit on the deck without the risk of fracturing our tailbones. So we grabbed and lurched and swore. Suddenly there was a cracking rattle of shrapnel on the bulkhead and dousing water on our necks.

"Get down! Squat!" yelled Farrell, and we bent down on our hunkers, grasping at each other's shoulders, at the bulkheads, at anything. That was the first mortar that came close. There were two more, and then the ping and whine of small arms in the air over us.

"Keep down!" yelled Farrell, with his head up over the bulkhead peering at the beach, "Still 300 yards to go."

We ground to a stop, after a thousand years, on the coarse coral. The ramp aft, seaward, cranked down fast and we tight-

The Beach –

My first view as I came around from the ramp of our LVT

PELELIU LANDING

ened our holds on our gear. The air cracked and roared, filled our ears and guts with its sound while Farrell bellowed, "OK! Pile out! Scatter! But follow me to the right! The right, goddammit, remember!" And we ran down the ramp and came around the end of the LVT, splashing ankle-deep up the surf to the white beach.

Suddenly I was completely alone. Each man drew into himself when he ran down that ramp, into that flame. Those marines flattened in the sand on that beach were dark and huddled like wet rats in death as I threw my body down among them. There was a rattle and roar under my helmet while I undid the chin strap and smelled the flaming oil and popping ammunition from the burning LVTs around us. Men of the first wave had penetrated about 25 yards inland as I looked up the sandy slope.

Then I ran—to the right—slanting up the beach for cover, half bent over. Off balance, I fell flat on my face just as I heard the *whishhh* of a mortar I knew was too close. A red flash stabbed at my eyeballs. About fifteen yards away, on the upper edge of the beach, it smashed down four men from our boat. One figure seemed to fly to pieces. With terrible clarity I saw the head and one leg sail into the air. Captain Farrell, near the burst, never dodged or hesitated but kept running, screaming at his men to follow him to their objective down the beach.

I got up to follow him, ran a few steps, and fell into a small shell hole as another mortar burst threw dirt on me. Lying there in terror, looking longingly up the slope to better cover, I saw a wounded man near me, staggering in the direction of LVTs. His face was half bloody pulp and the mangled shreds of what was left of an arm hung down like a stick, as he bent over in his stumbling, shock-crazy walk. The half of his face that was still human had the most terrifying look of abject patience I have ever seen. He fell behind me, in a red puddle on the white sand.

I ran farther to the right, angling up the slope. Suddenly I recognized Martin's big back (he was unarmed like myself) under a three-foot ledge on the upper rim of the beach where vegetation started. I made a final dash to throw myself under the ledge at Martin's side. The exertion was so great I fell down almost unconscious. When I opened my eyes again my throat burned, yet I was cold with sweat. We were lying with our heads to the ledge, not four feet from the aperture of a Jap "spider trap," a small machine-gun nest built into the face of the ledge with coco logs. Loose sand shovelled away from the aperture in two widening banks at either side made the trough in which we lay and gave additional cover. I wondered how well I could use my knife if a live Jap suddenly should poke an ugly face out at me from the opening formed by the logs.

Mortar shells whished and whapped through the air over our heads. They hit without apparent pattern on the beach and in the reef at our backs. Turning my head seaward I saw a direct center hit on an LVT. Pieces of iron and men seemed to sail slow motion into the air. As bursts began to creep steadily from the reef in toward the beach, the shells from one mortar rustled through the air directly over our heads at intervals of a few seconds, bursting closer, closer. Then a flat cracking flash nearly buried me with sand. Wriggling out, and trying to wipe the sharp grains from my sweating eyelids, I saw in the cling-

The Price

ing gray smoke that a burst had hit about six feet from my left foot, beyond the bank of loose sand at my side. In almost burying me, this sand had also saved me from shrapnel, except for one small piece that burned my left shin—which I did not know until later. I yelled to Martin, but he lay with face down, and did not answer. I could see no blood but I thought he was hit. A moment later he raised his head—I shouted, but he could not hear me. The blast had deafened him. Burst followed burst, creeping out to the reef and then back into the beach again. We hugged the earth and hung on.

Abruptly from close by, from over the ledge at our heads came a shuddering explosion, then a wild popping of .50-calibre shells. Later when we got up, we discovered an LVT on fire in the brush above us. It had run over a mine.

A different kind of shellburst began to come at us from a new direction. We judged it was 75-mm. artillery from a Jap battery down the beach on a peninsula to our right. We saw hits on five or six LVTs as they came jolting in over the reef. As I looked over my shoulder a burst smashed into a file of marines wading toward our beach from a smoking LVT. Jap machine guns lashed the reef with white lines and marines fell with bloody splashes into the green water. The survivors seemed so slow and small and patient coming in, out there.

Our carrier planes were swarming the sky again. Fighters roared in low over our heads almost continuously, strafing beyond our perimeter inland. Dive bombers peeled off by sections, dropping their 1000-pounders, and TBFs made their roaring rocket runs, finishing off with bellies full of 100-pounders for the Japs. We had it all our way in the sky over

Peleliu; there was not a Jap plane in the air. Airmen gave marines on Peleliu great support. Martin and I realized their efficiency and close contact with the ground command when we saw dive bombers making runs over the peninsula to our right. The Jap 75s were silenced.

For some reason mortar and sniper fire slackened too, and left us on our lonely beach in comparative quiet. We knew our lines were well toward the airstrip now.

Martin and I lay there weak, grateful and still, in the lull. Suddenly we were conscious of someone crawling up behind us from the beach, and we turned our heads. It was a corpsman. As we moved around to see him, he grinned and rasped, "Christ, I thought you were a couple of corpses!" We agreed.

The delicious lack of bursts in our immediate vicinity was like a life-renewing elixir. Tension broke for a few moments, and we lit cigarettes, the three of us. For myself, I was sampling the sheer joy of being alive.

The sector of the beach we could see from our trough in the sand was empty of living creatures. Two dead bodies and five wrecked LVTs were our closest company. I stared at the sand bank above my head and saw against the smoking sky the tangled, broken wrecks of coco palms and tropical trees with their big leaves hanging burned and dead. Two birds with long bills and short bodies lighted on a smashed palm frond and cried. Then the mortars started again.

Hugging the ground and turning our heads seaward, we watched the next wave of LVTs come in. They had good luck. I saw no hits. The amphitracks crawled in, pushed their snouts against the sand, and the men came up from the surf. Most of them streamed off to our right along the rim of the beach at the edge of the broken trees. Mortar fire shifted far to our left, and there was only the occasional zing of a sniper's bullet. Four men carrying posts and orange beach markers walked by, and another wave of LVTs discharged men along the whole length of the beach. We got up and started walking to our right. I remember the strange quietness, the dead marines in the white sand, the men with heavy loads trudging along in the smoke of the LVTs. Two rows of land mines, sown about six feet apart, lined our beach. The Japs had not tended them well; they were easy to see. We stepped carefully around their rusty bellies and forked horns.

Behind us came a burly man walking fast, as if on eggs. He bawled at the men he passed, "Where's the Seventh's CP?" and always got the reply, "Up that way, Colonel." We recognized him as the CO of our regiment, and fell in behind him, to find Farrell's bunch. When snipers' bullets and occasional mortar shells went over our heads on their way out to the reef, I instinctively pulled in my neck—though I could judge by now when they would be really close. It was interesting to watch the colonel ahead. He never bobbled or missed a pace, but there was plenty in his stiff stride—almost an expression on the back of his neck—to describe the trouble in his mind.

We followed him inland from the beach, plunging into the burned and twisted jungle trees. We stumbled through debris into an open space where four LVTAs were parked, and thirty paces farther into the trees we found our CP being set up in a trench dug by the Japs. It was six feet deep and about twenty yards long. Under our naval shelling the Japs had given it up just before we landed. Farrell had found it, cleared it of Jap machine-gun fire, and had it functioning as a command post when his superiors arrived. It was full of marines now, taking cover from sniper fire and mortars. A burst hit close at our backs just as Martin and I slid down into the trench. There was a yell for corpsmen—somebody was hit.

We sat in the trench, getting our breath. My legs trembled from exertion, but I felt very relieved, very secure. Out some 200 yards ahead, our front line inched forward and our perimeter grew more solid. Firing on our area slackened gradually.

By this time it was 1300. Some of us climbed out of the trench and walked back in the smashed trees to stretch our cramped legs. Disposal squads were working through the area, digging out dud rockets, bombs and shells. When a projectile could not be disarmed with tools, disposal men would explode it. They would clear the necessary area, pass the word loudly to get down, and let'er go—*blump!* All through the broken trees we found crude booby traps. Details were busy marking them and the land mines with red tape. Telephone linemen were unrolling their heavy spools of wire. Scout observation planes from warships wheeled high above our heads, directing naval gunfire. Occasionally they would go into a shallow dive and have awkward fun strafing.

Before noon the sun had bitten through the overcast of early morning and burned away all but a few white puffy clouds. Our planes were working against a background of bright, sharp blue. And as the sun, seven degrees above the equator, struck down upon us, it turned Peleliu into a bitter furnace.

PELELIU LANDING

Three of us had each carried a can of beer ashore in his pack. Giving each other the high sign, we gathered behind a broken palm log, punched holes with our knives in the three cans, and drank a toast, *To the Marines on Peleliu.* The beer was hot, foamy and wonderful. When it was gone, we were still dry-mouthed. And not a bit hungry.

About thirty paces back of the Jap trench a sick bay had been established in a big shell crater made by one of our battleship guns. Lying around it were pieces of shrapnel over a foot long. In the center of the crater at the bottom a doctor was working on the worst of the stretcher cases. Corpsmen, four to a stretcher, came in continually with their bloody loads. The doctor had attached plasma bottles to the top of a broken tree stump and was giving transfusions as fast as he could after rough surgery. Corpsmen plied tourniquets, sulpha, morphine, and handled the walking wounded and lighter cases with first aid.

The padre stood by with two canteens and a Bible, helping. He was deeply and visibly moved by the patient suffering and death. He looked very lonely, very close to God, as he bent over the shattered men so far from home. Corpsmen put a poncho, a shirt, a rag, anything handy, over the gray faces of the dead and carried them to a line on the beach, under a tarpaulin, to await the digging of graves.

It is hard to remember how the minutes ticked away, while the sun climbed down from the top of the blazing sky. The battle pounded on ahead of us. During flurries of fire I slid down into the trench; during the lulls I tried to find shade from the sun. I was without emotion of any kind. I saw everything

Sick-Bay in a Shellhole:
The Padre read, "I am the Resurrection and the Light."

around me in sharp focus, yet it no longer crashed into my consciousness. My mind blanked itself for my body's sake.

Our front advanced slowly, if at all; the radio in our trench picked up few reports, and the inactivity began to pall on Martin and me as we grew more and more curious about the battle's progress in other sectors. We had no access to the messages runners brought in to the colonel.

Farrell was sending two men to establish contact with the division command post which was supposed to be far down the beach to our left. Martin asked if we could go along and get news from the division command. We buckled our canteen belts and joined the two marines.

It is hard to walk through a jungle that has been subjected to saturation bombing and bombardment for a week. Jagged holes in the scattered stone and dirty sand, splintered trees and tangled vines made a churned, burned wilderness. Strewn through this chaos were not only the remnants and remainders of the marines' advance, but also the new men and new gear that had poured ashore to back up the front line. These men were digging in, making holes for themselves for the long night ahead when the Japs would surely counterattack. We jumped over foxholes, climbed over and around smashed trees, sidestepped tapes denoting mines and booby traps, walked gingerly around those yet unmarked. Telephone wires in crazy crisscross mazes were stretched along the broken ground. Scattered everywhere were discarded packs, helmets, rifles, boxes, clothes, rubber life belts—the rubbish of battle. Lying on the seared leaves and hot sand were dead bodies yet ungathered by corpsmen, the flesh bluish gray as the pitiless sun began to bring the peculiar and intolerable stench of human dead.

Planes came in strafing over our heads; the whump and chatter of firing to our right made a constant churning of sound. Sweat ran in streams from under our helmets which, without cloth covers, were burning to the touch. Our dungarees, wet with sweat, stuck to our legs and backs. The sand under our clothes scratched like sandpaper.

When we had snaked our way along for about 300 yards, the two marines with us began to ask the men we met where the division command post was. Nobody knew. We hunted for an hour, and never did find it. Intolerably hot and thirsty, Martin and I left the marines to their search. We turned left and walked down to the edge of the beach, planning to make our way back to our own CP by walking along the beach, the way we had first gotten there. The water's edge was crowded with men bringing equipment ashore.

We had walked fifty paces along the sand, dodging around LVTs, when we heard a mortar shell whirr over us and saw it send up its column of gray water about sixty yards out on the reef. That was the first of several salvos. They began to get hot.

We were passing by a big hole dug in the sand with a sign above it reading "Shore Party CP" when a burst hit about 25 yards down the beach at the water's edge, where we had been, and set an LVT on fire. We flopped into the very crowded Shore Party CP. The mortar fire lasted for about ten minutes, with most of the hits on that part of the beach we had just traversed. Later that evening we learned from the two marine messengers that in their further search for the division CP they had been directly under this fire and had four men killed in the same hole with them. They came back shaken and no longer eager.

Meanwhile we lay packed in the hole with the shore party. The supply officer in charge was stretched flat on his belly and holding a telephone in his hand. He wanted to make a call, but he would not get up to crank the box to get the operator. So I cranked it for him, as I was right by it. By the time he got an answer, and I had cranked and cranked, the mortar bursts were hitting farther down the beach away from us.

Some guy buried deep in the sand hole stuck his head up and began to gripe, "Goddammit, what are all you bastards in this hole for? Them bursts are a mile off. Scatter, you punks!" Just then a shell came whapping over and hit very close, and the guy buried his head again and said no more. Somebody grunted, "You're a brave son of a bitch walking around out there ain't you?"

In a few minutes Martin and I got up and continued our way down the beach through the welter of men, vehicles and ammunition cases. In some places things were so jammed up that we had to wade out into the surf to get around. The Jap mortars were far from silent, and direct hits on this kind of concentration really played hell. Yet regardless of fire, the marines were pouring everything they could get on the beach before nightfall and the expected counterattack. We watched sweating crews lift light artillery out of the amphitracks and haul them ashore. Martin muttered, "The more of those damn guns they put on here tonight the better I'll feel."

Turning in from the beach toward our CP we found the area thicker than ever with marines digging in for the night. There were foxholes every three or four feet, most of them barricaded with coral stones and logs moved around to help

PELELIU LANDING

deepen and strengthen the cover. The men worked at their places for the night earnestly, without much conversation except short declarations of fact: "It's the ferking night time I don't like, when them little ferkers come sneakin' into your lap." They dug in the dirt and cleaned their guns.

I saw a big redheaded sergeant I knew, lying in a hole with his eyes closed. It was his first action, and the day's events had bitten too deeply into his mind. At noon, I had seen him sink down on the ground with his hands over his face and cry.

We found our CP. The trench was twice as wide at the bottom as it had been, and cleared of broken tree limbs and big rocks. As we came up a bomb disposal officer was carrying out a dud rocket he had dug from the side of the trench. Improvements were going on. Marines were filling new gunnysacks, making sandbags to pile around the radio set and around the section of the trench where the colonel would spend the night. Men were hacking roots from the sides of the trench and smoothing out bumps, making places to rest their backs. Others were cutting poles from broken trees, laying them crosswise over their part of the trench, and tying their ponchos over the poles. It was getting cosy around the CP.

We asked Farrell if we could spend the night in the trench and he told us he had a place for us down at the extreme left end where he would be.

Very heavy firing suddenly started on our left. The radio operator got busy. When he finished writing out the message he showed it to us before he passed it down the trench to the colonel. It said our center was under heavy counterattack, the enemy using tanks. We knew we had three Shermans ashore, and sat there listening and hoping they would be enough. Gradually the firing died down. The attack stalled after the Shermans had knocked out eleven Jap tanks. A lull settled over us, as both sides prepared for the night.

About sundown we settled into our places at the end of the trench. The low sun cast a sulphurous yellow light through the smoke, then faded. Somewhat to the left and behind us two batteries of 75-mm. were placed. They fired a few rounds over our heads and the crack and blast made me jump. Then there was almost silence in the growing dusk. Our planes left the sky, heading out for their carriers. I got the orange and candy bar out of my pack, ate the candy, split the orange three ways to share with Martin and Farrell. Warm water from my nearly empty canteen was dessert. Word was passed that the "smoking lamp" would be out all night, that if anybody wanted a cigarette this was the last chance before morning. So we sat smoking in the dusk.

Martin and I spread a poncho under us and I hung my knife on a tree root over my head where I could reach it easily. We settled down to sleep, as close into Mother Earth as we could get. Mosquitoes began to swarm and bite. Like everyone else, I finally rummaged in my pack, found my headnet and gloves, and put them on.

We had expected that it might cool off after sundown, but we were wrong. With our headnets over our helmets and tied at the bottom around our necks, and with our gritty gloves on, we sat and steamed in puddles of sweat. Gun flashes occasionally silhouetted the top of the trench against the sky of misty stars. So began the long night in which the waking and the dozing nightmare merged.

PELELIU LANDING

A deep and numb kind of weariness both of body and of mind made the trench and the battle, the anxiety and uncertainty unreal, without the power of fact. I did not give a damn. I accepted each moment as it came, as if watching the paying out of a coiled cable, not being able to see when the end would suddenly come, time's end, world's end. Meanwhile the cable unwound. I was neither contented nor disturbed.

Little balls of fire danced under my eyelids when I closed my eyes. Flurries of gunfire rattled and thumped, and I seemed to be drifting off remotely into the sea of sound out there amongst the waves of a death I neither desired nor despised. Somewhere in those great waves was a peace that would lose me everything. Drifting out into the darkness farther, I struggled with those waves like a man on a life raft alone.

The blurred ring of the telephone about five feet from where I lay was like a tug at my sleeve, pulling me back to my fellows, back to my life, back from those huge waves of sound where I struggled alone. The quiet voice of the man on watch was crisp as he relayed information to the officers whose voices answered in the darkness down the trench. I could not help hearing what they said about weakness in our perimeter, about overextension of Baker Company, about lack of reserves, about failure to contact the Fifth, about our poor position for Jap counterattack. Hunched over in my hole, I had the dreamlike certainty that I was two people—one in a black pit who was too tired to live or die, the other standing by with a disembodied rather benign regret that living and dying were so similar and so confused.

Events were the only measurement of time as the night dragged on. I do not know what time it was when the counterattack came. There was a sudden flurry of rifle fire and blatting machine guns, a sudden pause, then a crashing answering fire from somewhere out in the blackness ahead of our trench. The phone rang. A battalion CO reported the Japs' infiltration and the beginning of the counterattack. He asked what reserves were available and was told there were none. Small arms fire ahead of us became a continuous rattle. Abruptly three star shells burst in the sky. As soon as they died floating down, others flared to take their place. Then the howitzers just behind us opened up, hurling their charges over our heads, shaking the ground with their blasts. Jap mortars spotted them, and bursts came our way. Some hit very close but I do not know what casualties they caused. The howitzer batteries answered every few seconds. The black air above our trench was gradually filled with the whistle and whine of small arms fire coming our way and crackling in the tattered brush over the banks of our trench. Our machine guns cracked in short deliberate bursts and were answered by the faster, higher chattering of the Japs' Nambus.

Then I heard, in pauses between bursts of fire, the high-pitched, screaming yells of the Japs as they charged, somewhere out ahead. The firing would grow to crescendo, drowning out the yells, then the sound would fall dying like the recession of a wave. Four times I heard the screaming Japs; in the firing I could not judge how near they came, though the second wave of yammering seemed closest. From down our trench in the lulls I heard our colonel giving orders to his operations officer who sat by another phone calling out to battalion commanders. Suddenly the colonel stood up and called for one of his

Counter attack.
The black well in the shaking earth
the BANZAI, the starshells

PELELIU LANDING

junior officers at our end of the trench. I heard him give orders to get forward every available machinegunner and rifleman from the rear of our position. A runner crawled out to pass the word. Small arms fire over our heads increased. A few moments later three riflemen on their bellies wriggled up behind the coco log that lay broken at the end of our trench about ten feet from where I sat, and started firing over the log. Looking up, I saw the earth, the splintered trees, the men on their bellies all edged against the sky by the light of the star shells like moonlight from a moon dying of jaundice.

I do not know how long it took the marines to beat the Japs back. Perhaps it was an hour, perhaps longer. If my weariness detached me from a sense of bodily peril, it also detached me from a sense of the passage of time. I floated calmly at the bottom of the black eternal well, strangely unconcerned with the fire and the sound that troubled its dark waters. There was no sudden cessation of battle; it slackened slowly. The words over the telephones were less frequent, the snapping whine of small arms became less steady, the artillery gradually ceased firing. Only the star shells kept going—like bursts of fever in the sky.

The borderline between sleeping and waking melted somewhere within this recession of battle. I dozed, feeling at the same time that I was awake, conscious of the hard stones against my back, the wet gritty sand against my skin, the aches in my bones, the dryness in my mouth. Yet I slept, I'm sure. Martin told me next morning that a foxlike creature with a bushy tail jumped into our hole, ran across my shoulder and up the sliding dirt at my back. I do not remember it. Yet I was awake later when Martin broke his snoring with a violent jerk and curse, and threw a land crab as big as his fist violently down the trench. It had pinched him on the backside and while he rubbed his behind and swore it seemed unbearably funny. I dozed again before daylight, for suddenly I opened my eyes and the sky was gray and the earth was silent. Quickly in the growing light the dark shapes of our trench acquired color, the three riflemen by the coco log grew sharp and clear.

The bottomless black well of night was a lie; the light of heaven had not forgotten us. The world lived again and so did we. Men stood up and grinned and perhaps were ashamed to speak their joy. Then from out of the silence there came a distant hum, growing steadily, becoming a roar. It was our planes: they had not forgotten either. As we climbed out of our trench men popped up out of foxholes everywhere like a magic army conjured from the debris of war.

The staccato rattle of strafing planes, the first rumbling blumps of the dive bombers began the second day of battle after the silence of dawn.

We wiped the slime off our front teeth and lighted cigarettes. Three of us shared our last orange, and I had a stick of chewing gum and the last water in my canteens for breakfast. Ground fire on our perimeter broke out again, and men buckled themselves for battle.

We learned more about what the Japs had done in the night. The nearest dead ones had been found about thirty yards in front of our position. They had infiltrated behind our perimeter, even stolen our aircraft markers and planted them far in our rear. There had been several charges—that explained the

Field Howitzer at edge of airfield.
Punching at 'Bloody Nose'

PELELIU LANDING

Banzai screams—but the marines had held them off in spite of thin spots in our lines. Japs wearing helmets of dead marines had sneaked into foxholes behind our front and cut throats. They had been slashed or shot by marines in hand-to-hand fighting in the darkness and there were bodies on the ground now in the morning light.

By 0800 our troops were beginning their day's push, with heavy air and artillery support. We knew the LVTs were pouring in over the reef again. The 105-mm. guns were at last being brought ashore and set up. The Jap mortars started again too, the bastards: corpsmen came in bearing the dead and the shattered.

Farrell turned to Martin and me. "I'm taking a patrol to see how things are going at the front. Would you like to go along?" We said we would, and a few minutes later we strung out in single file, with Farrell and eight of his marines, through the shattered jungle. We walked about 400 yards, skirting the airfield at its southern end.

This airfield was of course the prime reason for the Peleliu operation. It had big well-graded runways surfaced with finely crushed gravel. It danced now in the heat waves, wide and empty under the blistering sun. Although marines held two sides of the field, the Japs still commanded the 400-foot height along the left side and could, like the marines, register fire anywhere on the open space. It was no-man's-land that morning. Down at our end of the runway there was only one smashed Zero; up at the other end we could see big piles of wrecked Jap aircraft (117 by count later in the day).

At the southern end on our side of the field opposite the

hill our artillerymen had dug holes and carried 75-mm. field howitzers to the sites. As we came down to them these batteries were firing continuously, throwing shells into the Jap hangars and buildings at the foot of the hill, and at caves in the hill where Jap mortar and artillery and machine-gun fire was dealing out misery to marines. The targets were almost completely obscured by the smoke and dust of the shelling. A naval scout observation plane spotted fire for our batteries, and carrier aircraft strafed and dive bombed into the murk. Our patrol joined one of the 75-mm. gun crews for awhile, watching them fire. Farrell sent two of his scouts off into the mangrove swamps to locate a battalion commander whose outfit had taken the brunt of the Jap counterattack the night before. Farrell wanted his report for the regimental command. When the scouts returned and reported they had found him, we threaded our way into the tangled mangroves.

We found the battalion commander sitting on a smashed wet log in the mud, marking positions on his map. By him sat his radioman, trying to make contact with company commands on the portable set propped up in the mud. There was an infinitely tired and plaintive patience in the radioman's voice as he called code names, repeating time and again, "This is Sad Sack calling Charlie Blue. This is Sad Sack calling Charlie Blue—"

The whiskery, red-eyed, dirty marines sprawled around us were certainly sad sacks too. They had spent the night fighting in foxholes filled with stinking swamp water; they were slimy, wet and mean now.

The major was trying to establish the exact positions of

"This is Sad Sack calling Charlie Blue"

his companies before moving out of the miserable swamp closer to his day's objective. His people were taking some high ground to our right and had the job of smashing several big blockhouses and pillboxes overlooking the two peninsulas at the southeastern tip of Peleliu. Tanks and flamethrowers were spearheading the advance. We were in the swamp an hour before word came that the high ground had been taken.

As the battalion headquarters group prepared to move forward a supply detail came in carrying cans of water for the outfit. We each filled one of our canteens with the warm brackish stuff that sloshed from the square tins, and had a drink. Just as we were forming up to proceed toward the ridge the Japs laid their mortars and artillery on us. The nearest burst hit about twenty yards from where I ducked down, but the thick trees stopped the shrapnel and none of us was hurt.

There were about sixty of us, including Farrell's patrol. We started eastward in single file, three or four yards between each man, winding tortuously around muddy sink holes and uprooted trees and through the clinging network of vines and broken branches and seared leaves. Gradually we came to higher ground where bare stone sloped up in little ridges and defiles, and vegetation was not so thick. Sniper fire cracked in the trees above our heads, but we were not shelled.

As the sun climbed in the clear sky the heat grew. There was no breeze. Stinging sweat poured from our bodies and kept us wet in our muddy dungarees. That morning marines learned the full force of the sun on Peleliu, where coral rock bakes in the oven of the sky. The heat cut into our very marrow as we trudged up the ridge. The dead Japs we passed were

PELELIU LANDING

also affected by the heat; they had started to stink before they were stiff.

We could hear the heavy slugging of the tanks and mortars and howitzers, our crackling gunfire and the answering fire of the Japs just ahead as we came into an open pocket near the top of the gentle slope we were climbing. The clearing was a Jap barracks area surrounded by small pillboxes and antiaircraft positions. It was a smoking heap of rubble as we came into it. Everything in it was smashed, twisted, blasted. There were dead Japs on the ground where they had been hit and in two of the pillboxes I saw some of the bodies were nothing more than red raw meat and blood mixed with the gravelly dust of concrete and splintered logs. I felt no emotion except a kind of gladness that these bodies were dead. An occasional sniper bullet over my head gave some point to my gladness.

Over in some dry grass by a tree I stood a moment looking down at the face of a dead marine. He seemed so quiet and empty and past all the small things a man could love or hate. I suddenly knew I no longer had to defend my beating heart against the stillness of death. There was no defense. The burning hope of remaining restless, unwise and alive, forges frail armor for the beating heart.

The Japs had cleared a trail from their barracks to the top of a ridge where their strong points were. We walked carefully up the side of this trail littered with Jap pushcarts, smashed ammunition boxes, rusty wire, old clothes and tattered gear. Booby traps kept us from handling any of it. Looking up at the head of the trail I could see the big Jap blockhouse that commanded the height. The thing was now a great jagged

The Blockhouse and the Dead

lump of concrete, smoking. I saw our lead man meet a front line detail posted by the blockhouse while the other troops advanced down the hill with the three tanks and the flamethrowers. Isolated Jap snipers were at work on our slope; small groups of marines fanned out on both sides of the trail to clean them out, while we climbed toward the blockhouse.

To the left of the trail, about fifty paces from the summit, we came to an open-sided hut with a tattered palm-thatch roof, apparently the mess kitchen for nearby Jap installations. It was filthy and forlorn. Over the open fire pit hung three big blackened cooking pots, with nothing in them but a little charred stuff. On a dusty table were still strewn bright blue enamelware mess bowls with the Jap navy anchor printed on their sides. A big gunnysack of rice was broken and spilled in the dirt. I looked around for tinned crabmeat or *saki* but found nothing worth taking. The Japs had provided fine sanitary arrangements for their kitchen: under the same roof was a chicken roost and pig sty. The poultry was gone, but lying in the sty was a dead hog where a million flies were feasting. A marine came in from the trail and stopped at my side. Looking down at the pig in the puddle of blood, he shook his head and remarked, "Ain't it the goddamdest thing how a dead Jap looks exactly like a stuck hog?"

Just as we walked into the clearing around the blockhouse, a Jap sniper gave us a short machine-gun burst that splattered on the concrete over our heads. We all hit the dirt, most of us bunched up under the blockhouse walls. After a moment somebody got up and yelled, "All right you bastards—break it up and spread out." We did. The Jap did not risk another burst for awhile.

Heavy fighting was in progress just over the brow of the hill beyond the blockhouse clearing. Marine riflemen were still in position along the crest fifty paces ahead of us. Jap mortars from below occasionally overshot our front and burst on the hilltop. The area all around the blockhouse was still subject to sporadic fire and we did not loiter in the open places.

Among the scattered marines on the edge of the clearing I came face to face with a young lieutenant who had been a messmate of mine on the troopship coming to Peleliu. We had seen each other at dawn only the day before, yet we grinned, grimy and proud, as if we had not seen each other for years, shook hands and went our ways. Later I realized we had said a good deal with the handshake.

The battalion headquarters group turned right and went down the slope for better cover, to set up a command post in the trees. Soon Farrell and his men were the only marines left in the immediate area of the blockhouse.

In addition to its primary strongpoint, the hilltop clearing held two concrete pits about thirty feet in diameter constructed as mounts for heavy guns. Their circular walls slanted outward like saucers and around them were neatly painted 360-degree marks. Their decks were about eight feet below ground level and in the circular walls were cut entrances to caves which served as shelters for the gun crews. The pits had been tightly roofed over with brush camouflage now entirely burned off. We found not a trace of the big guns for which the pits had been constructed. Either bombing and bombardment had obliterated them or, more likely, they had never been installed.

Farrell and his patrol had numerous duties in the area, and

we sat in one of the gun pits for an hour, taking cover from Jap snipers and mortar fire while members of the patrol completed their work. Three of the six openings in the circular wall around us were blocked up with coral boulders. Peering in the caves behind the other three we found one was empty, another held two dead Japs. The last one, larger than the rest, was full of bloody bodies. They were piled up so tight it was hard to count them, but there were more than twenty. The marines were finding souvenirs, putting bloody Jap flags on the deck to dry in the sun, and examining the firearms and enemy gear scattered around us.

One marine found a beautiful and clean silk "belt of a thousand stitches." It was brilliant yellow with a purple rectangle at the middle top holding the embroidered name of the owner. Below the rectangle were ten lines of one hundred red stitches—little round red dots, embroidered. A thousand ladies had each sewn a stitch of well-wishing for the owner, but this feminine backing had done him damned little good. He was dead now and starting to stink there on the coral rock a long way from home.

The whole gun pit stunk, and the sun cut like a knife. I was glad when Farrell's patrol had covered the blockhouse area, and he decided to go forward, find a place on a ledge overlooking one of the peninsulas to the south, and observe the fighting. The marines were scheduled to take the peninsula that afternoon, but the Japs were putting up a bitter fight as they backed down the slope.

We made our way to the left side of the clearing where we cut into the woods. Then finding a narrow trace in the tangle

PELELIU LANDING

of trees, we followed it out to the eastern rim of the ridge. At one point a dead Jap lay on his back in the trace. Farrell bent over the body and saw a wire tight around the top of the right shoulder. He tried to peer around under the arm to see if a booby trap grenade was rigged in the armpit, but he couldn't tell. So he said to one of his marines, "We're going on. But go get one of the disposal men, and a line. Secure the line on this arm, get back plenty, and yank—to see if this son of a bitch is rigged. I think he is." I wanted to see that, but I went on with the patrol.

There were mines and booby traps all along the trace, but they were crude and easy to see. Farrell tore narrow strips off his white handkerchief and tied them on the stakes by the trip wires, to mark them for the troops that would come later.

The ledge where we came out, overlooking the beach and the peninsula to the south, had been strongly barricaded by a rough wall of coral boulders. Apparently the Japs had planned some additional work with reinforced concrete, for all along the inland side of the wall we found bundles of steel rods. At first we were careful about lifting our heads above the top of the wall, for now we were the extreme left flank of the marine front that bulged in the center down the hill to our right. After some experimenting, and drawing no fire, we poked our heads up and looked around at will. It was a ringside seat for the battle going on below us, for 400 yards, out to the peninsula's end.

We had been in our position for only a short while when the hot and heavy firing below us eased off into a lull. Farrell explained that the marines were drawing back to positions clear of the area where our aircraft and naval guns were scheduled to soften the Japs on the peninsula for the final ground assault.

While we waited for the fireworks, the sun started down its afternoon journey to the west. It beat upon us unmercifully. The shade from the scraggly brush over our position was thin; the glittering heat simmered us in our own sweat under our iron helmets.

Suddenly 8-inch shells from heavy cruisers started hitting from 250 to 400 yards ahead of us. They burst in tall sprays of flame and gray smoke. The very earth would tremble, and then we would hear the triple booming reports of the salvos. These giant fountains of flame spouted along the length and breadth of the peninsula again and again—then ceased as suddenly as they had begun.

Immediately from out of the sun dive bombers plummeted with the sound of some huge ripping fabric, as if they were tearing holes in the sky itself. We watched the black eggs leave the plane bellies, and as the divers pulled out and soared, the 1000-pounders would *blump* into the jungle. Over the peninsula there grew again high lazy trees of gray and mustard smoke, where seeds of fire had taken root.

Then torpedo bombers ran down the sky in steep slants, releasing their multiple rockets with a terrifying *whoosh,* and at the end of their runs dropping whole nests full of small black eggs that rattled in the air and roared as they tore into the earth. The torpedo planes did not soar out of their runs, but banked in tight turns and circled over us quite low. We could see their crews distinctly as they banked and peered down at us behind our wall. Two of the pilots waved.

Finally the fighters came, whole squadrons diving in by

sections, strafing. We watched the flaming orange paths of their tracers while the air was filled to bursting with the stuttering din of their guns.

The planes were hardly out of sight before the marines below us opened fire to advance. Down the slope the broken trees and the smoke obscured the actual movement of the troops. We could locate the fighting only by the new smoke puffs that rolled up out of the trees. Minute after minute the artillery and small arms slugged and pounded, and the firing positions did not change.

Suddenly Farrell cracked, "All right—you have targets—commence firing!"

We saw a Jap running along an inner ring of the reef, from the stony eastern point of the peninsula below us. Our patrol cut down on him and shot very badly, for he did not fall until he had run a hundred yards along the coral. A moment later, another Jap popped out running—and the marines had sharpened their sights. The Jap ran less than twenty steps when a volley cut him in two, and his disjointed body splattered seaward into the surf.

Our patrol was immensely cheerful when Farrell trained his binoculars and found the caves the Japs had run from. Other Japs were poking their heads out to fire, and for several minutes Farrell and his men peppered the cave mouths with M-1 and carbine bullets. The range was over 350 yards. I strained my eyes until they watered, trying to judge the effect of the firing. The marines claimed at least two more hits, but I did not see them myself.

While we kept our eyes peeled for more Japs, Farrell sent

War is Fighting and Fighting is Killing

one of his men back to the battalion CP to find out how the marine advance was going. About half an hour later he came back with salt sweat rolling over his cracked lips and reported that Jap resistance was very stiff, that our men were catching hell from pillboxes and gaining very little ground in spite of high casualties.

Farrell suggested that we might see more of the fighting under the ridge if we crawled over our wall and made our way down to the beach. Two marines, Farrell, Martin and I decided to go, leaving the rest of the patrol above to cover us.

We crawled over the tearing coral boulders and down the steep slope in the biting sun, heading for a rotten tree about ten feet from the water's edge. Farrell, Martin and I finally squeezed ourselves against the crooked trunk, both for cover and for shade. The two marines squatted by big stones nearby. I suppose we had been there between five and ten minutes, craning our necks at the fighting along the slope to our right—and not getting a very satisfactory view—when suddenly CRACK, a mortar burst hit on the beach to our left, and snipers' bullets splattered on the rocks at our backs. The fire came unexpectedly from the headland up north, toward which Japs from the caves had run. The mortar hadn't ranged us yet, and the riflemen were rotten shots, but we were in a very unhealthy place.

We scrambled up the slope and threw ourselves down between big rocks for cover. The heat between the stones out in the fiery sun was intolerable. As I lay there I grew dizzy and began to feel numb. I knew I had to move or I would faint. Without drawing another shot, I slid and crawled and wiggled back up the slope and over the wall. The other four men followed.

PELELIU LANDING

I flopped ten feet back of the barricade in a small patch of shade under some limp leaves. Our canteens had been empty since noon; I was very thirsty and infinitely tired. I lay there breathing fiery air over my dry teeth, wishing I had taken some training for this damned beachhead business.

Every few minutes a mortar would slam into the woods around us; stray rifle and machine-gun bullets sang and ricocheted in the brush over our heads. Down the slope to our right a couple of hundred yards I could hear our tanks trading wallops with Jap pillboxes. Fighter planes came in strafing with a razzle dazzle racket. I took it all for granted, more interested in my aches than in a battle. We waited for the front to advance so we could go down and have a look, but the front stalled, and the afternoon wore on.

About 1600 we heard marines talking as they came up the trace at our backs, then their voices were lost in the grinding and clanking of an LVT mashing a road up the trail we had travelled in the morning. Marines began to slouch by, loaded down with their packs and guns. Some of them went on over the ridge as reinforcements to the front; others filed down the ragged path back of our wall, and trampled through the brush up the slope at our backs. Farrell gave one man hell for stumbling by the strip of handkerchief tied as warning by a land mine about ten feet from where we were sitting. Marines were occupying our position in force to hold it during the night.

When I heard one of the new men say that the LVT had brought up some cans of water, I came to life immediately. I unbuttoned my canteens from my belt and without even putting on my helmet went off at a trot looking for the water cans. I spotted where the LVT had left them in a clearing at the top of the ridge and made for them. About fifteen paces from the water I nearly stepped in a big puddle of fresh blood. Looking up, I saw three marines carrying a man shot in the chest. They were taking him out of the clearing, and there was only one man standing at the water cans. I thought of nothing but getting some of that water and poured it into my canteens without saying a word to the other marine. A moment after I rejoined Farrell and Martin and we were drinking, a marine from our patrol came up puffing with his full canteen and said, "Goddammed snipers got two guys by me while I was pouring this. They got another guy just before that."

I drank several more hot swallows, feeling peculiar.

It appeared that the fighting was mostly finished for the day. Our perimeter for the night was being established; the troops around us were digging in. Farrell decided to go back to his regimental command and report.

Back in the blockhouse clearing we found two LVTs. One of them had brought up the water cans, the other had come up loaded with corpsmen, stretchers and first aid equipment. The coxswain of the one that had brought the water told us he was going to the beach and would take us. So we got in and grabbed hard to the bulkhead as we lurched away. The LVT slammed down the slope batting down trees, rocking over boulders, leaving a swath of churned hillside and dust. We came out of the brush near the southeastern corner of the airfield, rolled out into the open and headed for the end of the long runway on the southwest edge of the field. As we clanked and roared at our full speed of maybe twelve knots, I stood on an ammunition box to see out over the side and get a look at the scores of Jap aircraft smashed and burned on the ground.

PELELIU LANDING

Across the field to the northwest gray skeletons of hangars and barracks and the ruins of a little town lay dead at the foot of the highest hill on Peleliu. Incessant bombardment and bombing had chewed the western end off the ridge, burned from it the living jungle green, shattered its stone into ruinous sawtooth pinnacles and jumbled defiles. Gray against the smoky light of the slanting sun, it stood like the broken wilderness of a dead world. Yet within its crust were living Japs and chattering guns and the blood of dead marines was caked upon the hot and ghostly stone. The gunner of the LVT nudged me and pointed at the hill. "Bloody Nose," he said.

The chartmakers had marked it Umorbrogol Hill; marines had marked it now another way—and found its right name.

Past the howitzer batteries we had visited in the morning we turned into the jungle and found bulldozers scraping roads and carving clearings. The DUKWs were thick as ants, carrying supplies to dumps in the trees. Down on the beach where our LVT stopped at the water's edge, we got out to walk to our command post along the way Martin and I had first struggled on D-morning. Now it was totally unfamiliar, covered with vehicles and supplies and teeming with men. I felt lost in the maze of traffic, as if my memory lied about the lonely place under the terrible fire so long ago yesterday. Then a mortar burst hit close to the water's edge a hundred yards ahead, and made everything true again.

We got our packs at the CP and thanked Farrell and said goodbye. Marines chewing at K-rations looked up from the trench and did not hide their envy: "Hey, when you get back to that mudscow out there, will you go to the scuttlebutt and drink me about a gallon of that cold water?"

Down from BLOODY NOSE
Too Late
He's Finished - Washed Up - Gone

As we passed sick bay, still in the shell hole, it was crowded with wounded, and somehow hushed in the evening light. I noticed a tattered marine standing quietly by a corpsman, staring stiffly at nothing. His mind had crumbled in battle, his jaw hung, and his eyes were like two black empty holes in his head. Down by the beach again, we walked silently as we passed the long line of dead marines under the tarpaulins.

A DUKW picked us up and took us out to an LCVP. The sun was going down as we headed seaward. A mortar burst cracked on the reef like a last baleful word from Peleliu.